Also by Dr. Lynn Daugherty

Why Me?
Help for Victims of Child Sexual Abuse
(Even if they are adults now)

Voices of Survivors
Child Molestation Stories

Listening and Talking
to your Sexually Abused Child

Child Molesters, Child Rapists, and Child Sexual Abuse

Why and How Sex Offenders Abuse:

Child Molestation, Rape, and Incest Stories, Studies, and Models

by

Dr. Lynn Daugherty

Cleanan Press, Inc.
Roswell, New Mexico USA

Child Molesters, Child Rapists, and Child Sexual Abuse: Why and How Sex Offenders Abuse: Child Molestation, Rape, and Incest Stories, Studies, and Models

Print edition 1.0 (3/13)

Published by:

Cleanan Press, Inc.
106 North Washington Avenue
Roswell, NM 88203 USA

www.cleananpress.com

Acknowledgements

The classifications and descriptions of rapists and child molesters in this book are based on the work of Dr. Nicholas Groth and his colleagues. The concept of Child Sexual Abuse Accommodation Syndrome is based on the work of Dr. Roland Summit. The PHASE Typology for classifying adolescent sex offenders was developed by Dr. Michael O'Brien and Dr. Walter Bera. Dr. David Finklehor and his colleagues' Four Pre-Conditions Model of Child Sexual Abuse has provided an invaluable framework for understanding the occurrence of sexual abuse of children.

My husband, Larry Michelsohn, and my children, Moses and Aaron Michelsohn, have provided encouragement and support throughout this and all my other projects.

I am especially grateful to all the victims and abusers who have shared their stories and their struggles with me over the years.

Table of Contents

Warning—Disclaimer

Reading this book could bring on strong, unpleasant thoughts and feelings. These could even lead to thoughts of suicide or other injury to self or others. If you find yourself overwhelmed by these thoughts or feelings, please seek professional mental health services immediately!

This book is not intended to replace the services of a professional mental health counselor, or to provide professional psychological services to you. If you need expert professional help, you should seek the services of a competent mental health professional.

Every effort has been made to make this book as accurate as possible. However, mistakes, both typographical and in content, may occur. Furthermore, this book contains information that is current only up to the date of publication. Therefore, this text should be used only as a general guide to understanding child sexual abuse and abusers and not as the ultimate source of information. Please learn as much as possible about child sexual abuse and abusers from all available sources and tailor the information to your own individual needs.

The author and Cleanan Press, Inc. shall have neither liability nor responsibility to any person or entity with respect to any loss or damage caused, or alleged to have been caused, directly or indirectly, by the information contained in this book.

Introduction

Widespread public awareness of child sexual abuse has only begun to develop during the last few decades. Even experts in the field are just beginning to study it carefully.

Many questions about child sexual abuse do still remain unanswered. Yet with time, definitive answers will be discovered.

Fortunately, much information is already available. Current studies and research provide at least some answers to some questions that more and more people are asking right now:

What is child sexual abuse? How common is it? Who are its victims? (Chapter 1)

How can child sexual abuse take place? (Chapter 2)

Who are these people who abuse children sexually and why do they do it? (Chapter 3-8)

Can child sexual abusers stop abusing? (Chapter 9)

This book is written to provide you—a parent, a former victim, a mental health professional new to the field, or a concerned member of the general public—with a basic understanding of how and why child sexual abuse takes place in our world today, and to give you insight into some of the motivations that lead people to abuse children sexually.

A Note about the Stories of Abuse: Only *actual personal stories of victims and abusers are included in this book. They are selected to illustrate various types of abuse and abusers. Some details of the stories have been changed to protect the privacy of the individuals involved. When a particular type of abuser or abuse is not illustrated with a story, it is because the author never encountered that particular type of abuser in her practice of psychology.*

Chapter 1.
Facts About Child Sexual Abuse

These are common basic questions about child sexual abuse:

What is sexual abuse?

Sexual abuse takes place any time a person is tricked, trapped, forced or bribed into sexual activity. It most often involves unwanted touching of the victim, but can involve any of a wide variety of sexually motivated activities.

Why is sexual abuse wrong?

Sexual abuse is wrong because it hurts people! Sometimes it hurts the victim physically. More often it causes the victim to suffer psychologically. It can cause fear, confusion, anger, shame, depression and lowered self-esteem for the victim. These can lead to other serious problems later in life.

Each person's body is private and belongs to that person alone. Each person has the right to decide who may touch his or her body, when it may be touched, and how. Sexual abuse violates the right of each person to make important decisions about his or her own body.

What is the difference between sexual abuse and "normal sex play?"

It is normal for children to explore their own and other children's bodies and for children to touch their own bodies or those of other children in ways that feel good. This "normal sex play" is one way we learn about our bodies and our own likes and dislikes. It is also one way we learn about the bodies of other people.

Sexual abuse is different. It involves sexual contact that is tricked, trapped, forced or bribed. Usually the abuser is older, more knowledgeable, or more powerful than the victim and takes advantage of this difference.

What happens during child sexual abuse?

Sexual abuse may include any type of sexual activity. It can range from forcible rape to gentle but unwanted touching. Being unwillingly exposed to the genitals of another or forced to show one's own genitals to someone else is also a form of sexual abuse. Involving a child in pornography or prostitution constitutes sexual abuse, as well.

Are boys ever sexually abused?

Both boys and girls are victims of sexual abuse although girls are probably victimized more frequently. Approximately ten percent of all victims reporting sexual abuse are boys, but probably many more are abused.

Who sexually abuses children?

Children are usually abused by someone older than themselves. Often the person is in some position of authority over the child. This may be an adult stranger, a parent or step-parent, an aunt or uncle, a grandfather or grandmother, a teacher, a spiritual counselor, or an adult friend. It may even be a teenage babysitter, an older cousin, an older child in the neighborhood, or an older brother or sister. Four out of five child victims are sexually abused by someone they know and trust, rather than by a stranger.

How does child sexual abuse happen?

Although violent sexual attacks on children sometimes take place, the sexual abuse of children usually involves more subtle force. This may be threats of harm or threats of "telling on" the child for some misdeed. Other times the child may be bribed with gifts or special privileges. In some situations the child may simply want to please or appease the abuser.

Children are often tricked into unwanted sexual contact. This may involve games that start out as fun and end with unwanted contact. Sometimes the older person tricks the child by telling him or her that what they are doing is "okay" or that "everybody" does it, or that it is for the child's own good, or for his or her education.

The sexual abuser's power, knowledge, and resources are greater than those of the child victim. The abuser uses this difference to take advantage of the child.

What different patterns of child sexual abuse occur?

Child sexual abuse can be divided into three patterns that may have different effects on the victim.

Brief incidents of abuse

This type of sexual abuse happens as an isolated incident. While this type of abuse is often perpetrated by the stereotypical "dangerous stranger," the abuser may also be an acquaintance. A stranger may expose his genitals to a child who is walking down the street. An acquaintance may try to touch the child's genitals while in a movie. A child may be kidnapped and raped. Both boys and girls are commonly the victims of brief incidents of sexual abuse.

From a female victim of a brief incident of abuse:

I was just starting to develop. One day I was riding the subway with my mom at rush hour and it was packed. Suddenly I realized the guy next to me was feeling me up. I just froze. He looked me right in the eyes and grinned, and kept doing it. I didn't know what to do. My mom was right there but I was too shocked and embarrassed to say anything. I didn't want her or anybody to know, and she never did. I felt trapped, pushed up against him. I just stood there frozen until he got off at the next stop. I still feel dirty when I think about it.

Abuse in a continuing relationship

This type of sexual abuse occurs as part of an ongoing trusted relationship. The abuser may devote considerable time to developing the relationship, a process sometimes called "grooming" the child (and the family) for future abuse. This typically involves developing the trust relationship while also introducing the child to innocent activities that set the stage for later abuse. An example might involve the abuser casually putting an arm around the child in front of the parents, then hugging ever more intimately in private. The abuse usually starts gradually and continues for weeks, months, or years. The abuser may be a neighbor who invites the child to his or her house to play regularly. It might be a teacher, camp counselor, physician, priest, or family friend. The victim may be a boy or a girl.

From a male victim of abuse in a continuing relationship:

I think Father Angelo was really a little senile. I was only about five and he would take me on his lap whenever he came to our house to sit by my grandmother's bedside. She was pretty out of things and died not long afterwards. He would wrap his arms around me and rub my crotch while he recited prayers. I'm not sure where my parents were during his visits but it was just me and him and my nonna in her bedroom. It seemed like a real special time. It wasn't until I was much older that I realized this wasn't right. By then he had died too.

Incest

In this type of sexual abuse, the abuser is a member of the child's immediate family, most often a stepfather or older brother. The victim is usually a girl but boys are also victimized through incest. The abuse usually begins gradually but happens more often as time goes on. The abuse may continue for years until someone outside the family discovers it or until the child grows up and leaves the house.

From a female victim of incest:

My older brother used to do it with me. At first I didn't know any better. He would say "You're going to play with my thing," and I would until it got real stiff. Then he would say "Now I'm going to play with your thing," Of course I didn't have a "thing" but he would rub me down there. It was a fun secret game, just between us. Later, when I started to see it wasn't normal, he threatened to tell Mom I'd done something bad if I didn't play, or if I told anybody. This went on until he finally left home when I was about 10.

How do people use the Internet to abuse children sexually?

Some abusers find their victims on the Internet. They use chat rooms or social media websites to meet children and gain their trust. Then they may exchange sexual messages or pictures with their victims, or arrange face-to-face meetings to abuse them.

Abusers who exploit children through prostitution or pornography sometimes use the Internet to find other abusers who will use their services. They also use the Internet to find children to abuse through prostitution or pornography.

Some abusers use the Internet to meet other abusers. They share their views about child sexual abuse, ideas about how to find and abuse children, information about specific victims, or suggestions about how to avoid being caught or punished for their crimes.

How many children are victims of sexual abuse?

Statistics suggest that as many as one child in four in the United States becomes the victim of sexual abuse by the time he or she reaches the age of 18. This means that at least 25% of American adults were victims of child sexual abuse. Child sexual abuse is a very common problem around the world and is even more common in countries with unstable political or social environments.

The information presented in this book was collected in the United States, but studies suggest that much of it also applies in other countries.

At what age are children usually abused?

Children may be abused at any age from infancy to adolescence. The most common age for sexual abuse to begin is age nine. Most sexual abuse is reported by teenagers, but they have usually been victimized for many years before finally reporting it. Most sexual abuse, particularly that involving a continuing relationship or incest, starts before the child reaches puberty.

What do research studies tell us about the risk factors for being sexually abused as a child?

Research studies have been useful in identifying specific risk factors that increase a child's chances of becoming a victim of child sexual abuse. It must be kept in mind that these "risk factors" do not "cause" sexual abuse. They only allow the sexual abuse to take place once the potential abuser is ready to abuse.

First of all, studies indicate that some factors often considered do not increase the risk of child sexual abuse. No difference in rates of abuse between African-Americans and Caucasians have been identified, and no difference between upper and lower socioeconomic groups have been found. Child sexual abuse seems to occur equally among socioeconomic groups. Religion, family size, and home crowdedness are also factors that have not been found to be related to the risk of child sexual abuse.

A number of background factors do seem to be clearly associated with higher risk of sexual abuse. Girls are at a higher risk than are boys. Children ages 8 through 12 are at a higher risk than either younger or older children. Girls with few friends in childhood are more often victims, but this may be an effect of the abuse itself.

17

Research studies suggest that the strongest and most consistent risk factors involve the parents of abused children. Children most at risk, especially girls, are those who have lived without their biological fathers in the home, whose mothers worked outside the home, whose mothers were disabled or ill, who witnessed conflict between their parents, who had a poor relationship with one of their parents, or who lived with stepfathers. Some studies suggest that the rate of sexual abuse among Hispanics may be slightly higher than that among Caucasians or African-Americans, and that the rate of sexual abuse among Asian-Americans may be slightly lower.

It makes sense that family variables may be highly important risk factors for a child. When a child is missing a parent, has a poor relationship with a parent, or has parents who are in conflict with each other, the child may be less well supervised. A poorly supervised child is less protected from potential abusers. Additionally, a child with poor relationships with his or her parents may be unhappy or emotionally needy. The child may then be more vulnerable to an adult abuser. The child may welcome the friendship, appreciation, gifts, or promises of the abuser. The child may be less self-confident and less able to stand up for him or herself in any situation, and thus less able to resist abuse. The child may also be afraid to tell his or her parents about the abuse because of lack of support from them.

The strongest risk factor identified for girls is the presence of a stepfather in the family. Shockingly, studies suggest that as many as 50% of all girls who grow up with a stepfather are sexually abused. Often, the stepfather is not the abuser, however, but rather the circumstances that led to there being a stepfather present, such as those mentioned above. The girl may have been abused before the stepfather entered the home. While a mother is dating, a variety of potentially abusive men have access to her children. Of course, a potentially abusive stepfather is also in a position to abuse the girl easily. Additionally, he may have friends who attempt to abuse the child because she is "not really" his daughter.

In spite of girls' greater risk, boys often become the victims of child sexual abuse. It is difficult to know exactly how many boys experience child sexual abuse, however. Probably fewer boys than girls are abused sexually. Certainly, fewer boys report abuse. Boys are more likely to be abused by individuals outside of the family than by family members. Boys, like girls, are primarily abused by men.

Unlike girls who are sexually abused, boys who are sexually abused are likely to come from lower socioeconomic groups and families where physical abuse is present. For boys, physical and sexual abuse are more commonly found together. When a boy is sexually abused by a family member, that family member is very likely to be abusing other children in the family as well, especially girls. Boys victimized alone are more likely to be victims of non-family members and are generally younger than other victimized children.

Why doesn't the child victim always report being sexually abused?

Children have many reasons for not reporting that someone has sexually abused them. The very young child may not realize that the abuser is doing anything wrong. Children are taught to obey adults. The child may not realize at first that he or she should object.

Later the child may not tell anyone because of fear. He or she may fear the abuser or fear not being believed. The child may fear that he or she will be punished or blamed for the abuse or that some harm will come to the abuser. The victim of incest may fear that the family will be broken up if anyone finds out about the abuse. Then he or she may work very hard to keep it a secret.

Some children keep the sexual abuse a secret because they enjoy the affection or attention that goes along with it. Another reason that children don't tell anyone they have been sexually abused is because of their own feelings of shame and guilt. Child victims often believe that somehow the abuse is their fault and marks them as "bad" or "different." They try to keep others from finding out how "bad" they are.

Sometimes when children try to report sexual abuse, they are not believed or are "hushed up." They may give up trying to tell anyone else. This is especially true if it is a parent who does not believe the child.

What is Child Sexual Abuse Accommodation Syndrome?

American psychiatrist Roland Summit described a pattern of seemingly contradictory behavior often seen in victims of child sexual abuse and called it Child Sexual Abuse Accommodation Syndrome.

This syndrome describes a common pattern of reactions of children who are victims of incest. The reactions are all the normal responses of normal children who are sexually abused but are different from what other people expect. The difference between how a child reacts normally and how people expect a sexually abused child to react often makes it harder for the child to be believed if he or she finally does report the sexual abuse.

At first the child victim keeps the sexual abuse secret because of confusion, fears, and feelings of guilt and shame. The child feels helpless, powerless to stop the sexual advances of an adult that he or she depends on. So the child does nothing, often pretending to be asleep in bed at night while the abuse takes place.

As the abuse continues the child adjusts to it and is trapped by it. The child comes to believe that he or she is the guilty person who deserves to be punished by the abuse. It becomes the victim's duty to keep the family together by submitting to the abuse and keeping it a secret.

Finally, often after many years of abuse, the child may report it. This often comes after a fight with the abuser. Then the authorities do not believe the child's claim of being abused. The secrecy, helplessness, immobility, and the adjustments the child has made do not seem like normal reactions to other people. Therefore, they often do not believe that sexual abuse could have taken place the way the child claims.

If the child is believed, he or she is often the one removed from the home. Many times criminal charges are not brought against the abuser because there is not enough proof. As a final step, the victim is often pressured by family members to take back the claims of abuse. The child gives in to the pressure and recants, changing his or her story. This lie is quickly believed.

This Child Sexual Abuse Accommodation Syndrome is seen in many cases of father-daughter incest. Some of its elements can also be seen in other types of incest or other patterns of sexual abuse.

Unfortunately the concept of Child Sexual Abuse Accommodation Syndrome, which is useful in understanding some seemingly contradictory behavior in abuse victims, has sometimes been used improperly in prosecuting accused child sexual abusers. The existence of Child Sexual Abuse Accommodation Syndrome has been used to argue that if a child reports being abused, this is (of course) evidence of abuse, and if a child denies being abused this is also evidence of abuse.

Do people ever forget being sexually abused as children, and then later remember these experiences?

One way the human mind protects itself from overwhelming emotional pain is by "forgetting" (repressing) bad memories. People who have been through extremely frightening or painful experiences, like wartime combat, natural disasters, torture, or sexual abuse, sometimes "forget" these experiences.

Later these painful memories may come back. This most often happens when the person finally feels strong enough to deal with the emotional pain of the traumatic event.

Can people ever have "false memories" of child sexual abuse?

People often remember the details of their experiences incorrectly. Sometimes people "remember" events that they imagined, or that someone convinced them really happened when it didn't. Although some people disagree, nearly all mental health professionals believe that most memories of child sexual abuse are true and generally accurate, however.

Is there a typical pattern of sexual abuse?

Sexual abuse in incest and in other continuing relationships usually follows a predictable pattern. First of all, the abuser finds a way to be alone with the child and to gain the child's cooperation. This allows the abuser to begin sexual activity with the child. The sexual activity usually becomes more frequent and more intimate over the time.

Once sexual activity begins, the abuser tries to make the child keep it a secret. This secrecy phase may last for weeks or months or years.

Although most child sexual abuse is never revealed, sometimes it is accidentally discovered or disclosed on purpose. If the victim receives good support, the full story may come out and the victim can receive help. However, some families discourage the victim from cooperating with authorities. The victim may be pressured to downplay the abuse and its effects. Under pressure from the abuser or the family, some victims even deny that the abuse occurred.

Why do people sexually abuse children?

Sexual abusers usually don't want to hurt the children they abuse. In fact, they often like children and try to please them. Many times abusers don't realize how much harm their behavior causes.

Many abusers are very self-centered people who have trouble considering anybody's welfare but their own. Because they enjoy the sexual activity, they believe the children do as well. Some abusers, because of their own selfishness, just don't care whether they harm the child or not.

A small number of abusers achieve pleasure or satisfaction from hurting others, including children. Occasionally people with serious mental or emotional illnesses abuse children because they do not recognize that their actions are wrong.

Most sexual abusers have trouble relating to people their own age. Because they are often afraid or insecure in relationships with people their own age, they turn to children for companionship, friendship and sexual gratification. They feel safer and more comfortable in relationships with children. Children are more trusting and easier to please than other adults, as well as being easier to dominate.

Most people who sexually abuse children are not "crazy," but they do have serious psychological problems. They need help with these problems. Many sexual abusers were victims of sexual abuse themselves as children.

Is the child victim to blame for the sexual abuse?

No! Even though many child victims feel guilty about being sexually abused, what happened was not their fault. This is true even if the child did do something else wrong that resulted in abuse, such as getting in a car with a stranger or engaging in some other risky or forbidden activity. The abuser is totally responsible for his or her own behavior.

Can a person who was sexually abused ever lead a "normal" life?

Yes! Most victims of child sexual abuse go on to lead very normal lives. They usually function well in most areas of everyday life. Victims of child sexual abuse have gotten themselves through some very tough situations. This is a real accomplishment! Such victims have important strengths.

Most victims of child sexual abuse make successful lives for themselves in spite of the hardships they have suffered. Remember, at least 25% of adults in America today were victims of child sexual abuse. That's 25% of doctors, lawyers, actors, teachers, bus drivers, miners, politicians, plumbers, forest rangers, social workers, homemakers, yoga instructors, lab technicians, fry cooks, realtors, tennis pros, astronauts, bartenders, and Walmart greeters.

However, the effects of child sexual abuse usually make their lives more difficult in some ways. Many times former victims do not realize that some of the problems they are having in their present lives are really the result of having been sexually abused as children. Once they realize this, working out the problems becomes easier. Even those having more serious problems can usually be helped by a professional counselor, and they can greatly improve their own lives.

Chapter 2.
A Model for Understanding Child Sexual Abuse

Many people have tried to understand and explain why child sexual abuse takes place. Some focus on personalities of the abusers or victims, while others point to biological factors or to pressures within our society.

It is always difficult to explain "why" anything happens. Right now we have many theories about child sexual abuse but we have even more questions. No one really knows "why" child sexual abuse takes place. However we do know what conditions are necessary for child sexual abuse to occur, thanks to a group of researchers at the University of New Hampshire.

The Four Pre-Conditions Model
Of Child Sexual Abuse

American sociologist Dr. David Finkelhor and his colleagues have proposed a comprehensive model that identifies four necessary factors that must be present for child sexual abuse to take place. This model gives us a basis for understanding child sexual abuse more clearly and is also helpful in designing interventions to prevent child sexual abuse.

Dr. Finkelhor calls each of the four factors necessary for child sexual abuse to take place a "pre-condition." When all four pre-conditions are present, child sexual abuse occurs. When any one of the pre-conditions is missing, child sexual abuse cannot occur.

In Dr. Finkelhor's model, two of the pre-conditions relate to the potential abuser while two relate to the potential victim.

Abuser Pre-Conditions

Pre-Condition 1: The potential abuser must have some motivation to have sex with the child.

A potential abuser must want to have sex with a child in order for child sexual abuse to take place. This desire is not necessarily unusual. Repeatedly, studies show that many (if not most) of us as adults feel inclined toward sexual activity with a child (someone under the age of 18) at some time or another. (Of course, most of us never act on this inclination.)

This motivation to have sex with a child may come from any of several sources.

Some people are motivated to have sex with children because they are sexually aroused primarily by children. Children are their "first choice" for sexual partners. They have sex with children because their interests are "fixated" or "stuck" at early levels of psychosexual development and they find children more sexually exciting than adults.

Innate biological factors such as hormonal or genetic problems that we don't yet understand may make some individuals more easily sexually aroused by children than by adults.

Other men and women may have learned to become sexually aroused by children. This may have developed because of early sexual experiences with other children or because of child pornography or advertisements that portray children in sexual ways. They may have learned only too well what our society teaches, that the most desirable sexual partners are youthful and subservient.

Other people may mistake strong emotional feelings for children as "sexual" when others would identify them as "affectionate" or even "parental."

Other potential abusers may prefer sexual activity with adults, and only turn to children as a "second choice" to meet their sexual needs when adult sexual partners are less available or are less satisfying at the moment. These people "regress" in their sexual interests and have sex with children as an alternative way of achieving sexual gratification.

Repressive teachings about sex, early unresolved conflicts regarding parental figures, traumatic sexual experiences with other adults, blows to self-esteem, or lack of social skills can all cause a man or woman to avoid social or sexual relationships with other adults temporarily or permanently. Instead, they turn to children, whom they find less threatening.

Still other potential abusers may be trying to satisfy important emotional needs which have nothing to do with sex itself: needs to be liked or needs for excitement or needs to express anger or to feel powerful or needs to be in control of another person. Some potential abusers may try to fulfill these emotional needs through sexual activity with children, often because, once again, children are less threatening to them.

Any of these motivations may lead a potential abuser toward sexual activity with a child. Often elements of several types of motivation, in varying degrees, lead the man or woman toward such activity.

Pre-Condition 2: The potential abuser must overcome his or her own inhibitions against sexual activity with a child.

While many of us think about sexual activity with a child at one time or another, few of us abuse children sexually. Thinking about sexual activity is vastly different than having sex—certainly as far as it affects the child!

Most potential abusers have inhibitions against sexual activity with a child. For some of us, this comes from beliefs that sexual activity with children is wrong. For others of us, it comes from fear of being punished if caught. For most of us, most of the time, even if we are interested in having sex with a child, our inhibitions against this type of behavior are stronger than our motivations to engage in sexual activity with a child.

For child sexual abuse to take place, a potential abuser must find a way to overcome whatever internal forces stop him or her from having sex with a child.

What motivations can be strong enough to overcome these inhibitions?

Most potential child sexual abusers, like all of us, have a variety of emotional and sexual needs. Lack of other ways to satisfy emotional or sexual needs can lead a person to sexual activity with a child. Long-term social isolation, poor social skills, or frustration in interpersonal relationships that create pressures from longstanding unmet needs may push a person to consider the "easier" approach of meeting needs by having sexual activity with a child.

High levels of stress can also work to overcome inhibitions against child sexual abuse on a short term basis. Stress makes it difficult to think clearly, and also makes us uncomfortable in physical and psychological ways. Then pressures to satisfy sexual or emotional needs can overpower normal inhibitions.

Some abusers who normally have adequate inhibitions against child sexual abuse may reduce their inhibitions against child sexual abuse temporarily (either intentionally or unintentionally) by using alcohol or other drugs.

Psychological mechanisms such as "denial" or other ways of hiding the truth from ourselves ("It isn't really wrong, just this once, because . . .") may also make it possible to overcome normal inhibitions against having sex with a child.

The influence of society can strengthen or weaken an individual's inhibitions against child sexual abuse. Society reduces inhibitions against child sexual abuse when it tolerates or encourages sexual interest in children, such as through child pornography or child prostitution. Society also reduces inhibitions against child sexual abuse when criminal sanctions against child sexual abuse are weak or uncertain.

Other processes can interfere with inhibitions against child sexual abuse. Some potential abusers have serious mental or emotional problems that disrupt their thinking and reduce their ability to control their behavior appropriately. Mental retardation, brain damage (resulting from accident or disease), or other serious mental problems such as schizophrenia, can lead to problems with judgment and behavioral controls that reduce a person's inhibitions against sexual activity with children. Most individuals with these problems do not abuse children, however.

Other potential abusers have very few internal inhibitions against the idea of sexual activity with children. For these people, the fear of punishing consequences if they get caught forms their primary inhibition against sexual activity with a child.

Some of these people having few inhibitions against sexual activity with children are sociopaths, sometimes described as having "no conscience." They do not care about any rules of society that interfere with their own desires and pleasures. Others, who do have consciences, may have trouble recognizing or believing that child sexual abuse can cause children harm. Still others may truly believe that sexual activity with children is appropriate under certain conditions.

Victim Pre-Conditions

Once a potential abuser wants to become sexually involved with a child and has found a way around his or her own inhibitions, two of the four pre-conditions necessary for child sexual abuse to occur have been met. The other two pre-conditions relate to the victim.

It is extremely important to remember, however, that even though two "victim factors" play a role in allowing child sexual abuse to take place, total responsibility for the abuse remains with the abuser. If the first two pre-conditions— the abuser's motivation to abuse a child and his or her ability to overcome any internal inhibitions against it— were not present, the victim factors would not matter!

Pre-Condition 3: The opportunity to engage in sexual activity with the child must arise. The potential abuser must have a chance to be with the potential victim, usually alone.

A potential abuser and a child must have the chance to be together for child sexual abuse to occur. Physical separation of the child from others (except the abuser) is usually necessary for abuse to occur. Child sexual abuse usually occurs when an abuser is alone with a child (either in the real world or in a virtual world such as on the Internet), thus time a child spends away from appropriate supervision provides the potential for abuse.

Lack of supervision of a child is a primary factor leading to opportunity for that child to become a victim of child sexual abuse. Supervision does not simply mean being with a child physically at all times. It includes knowing what is happening with the child, especially when the child is troubled. It also includes having a good relationship with the child and being physically and emotionally available to the child in times of need.

Emotional or social isolation can play an important role in giving a potential abuser access to a child. A child who is physically or emotionally "alone" is more easily accessible to a potential abuser.

Mothers appear to be especially crucial in protecting children from child sexual abuse, perhaps because mothers remain the primary caretakers for most children. Abuse is more likely to occur to children if their mothers are absent or ill. Abuse also happens more often to children whose mothers are not close to them emotionally or who are not protective of them. A mother who herself is dominated or abused by a potential abuser often leaves her children open to abuse.

A potential abuser must find an opportunity to have access to the child if child sexual abuse is going to occur. Generally, the type of access a potential abuser has determines the type of abuse that can take place. Different types of physical and emotional access lead to brief incidents of abuse, to abuse in a continuing relationship, or to abuse through incest.

In a brief act of child sexual abuse, this opportunity may be as simple as finding a child alone momentarily away from other children or adults.

Opportunity may also involve getting close to the child emotionally. If a potential abuser is part of a continuing relationship, the abuser may have already gained the trust of the child and parent through the "grooming" process. This allows opportunities for being physically alone with the child with little danger of interruption or discovery.

Opportunity for an incestuous relationship to develop is readily available within a family, especially when communication among family members is limited or relationships are distant. This may happen if one or both parents are often physically absent from the home. Frequent opportunities for a potential abuser to be alone with a child, particularly when there is lack of contact with another adult, can lead to abuse. Physical conditions, such as sleeping arrangements, can also be factors.

Pre-Condition 4: The resistance of the child to the sexual activity must be overcome. The potential abuser must find a way to get around whatever resistance the child presents.

Children do have some capacity to avoid or resist abuse, and often do so. Most children have a difficult time resisting the advances of a potential abuser, however. They are usually at a disadvantage in the contest because of the greater knowledge, power, or authority of the potential abuser.

Overcoming a child's resistance may involve purely physical strength, as in the case of forcible rape. Or it may involve verbal force. Threats from an adult can create fear in a child, or a child may simply assume that such threats are implied. These fears may range from fear of physical harm (to the child or to others) to embarrassment, shame, fear of hurting others emotionally, or to fear of losing valuable companions or family members physically (by being taken to jail) or emotionally (by being angry at the child).

More often, efforts to overcome resistance are more subtle. A potential abuser may use attention, trust, or superior knowledge to manipulate a child into sexual activity by taking advantage of his or her need for attention, love, or companionship.

Some children are more easily victimized than others. A potential abuser may select a particular child because of subtle cues related to that child's situation, personality, behavior, or self-confidence indicating that this child's resistance may be easier to overcome.

An emotionally needy child will be much more vulnerable to the offers of attention, affection, or bribes, than a child who is confident of the love and concern of others. A child who is emotionally abused or neglected or who has poor relationships with his or her parents becomes more vulnerable to abuse. Children who are young, naïve, or who lack information are also at a greater risk.

Some children, especially younger children, may not know that sexual activity with an abuser is wrong. Others may sense that something is wrong but accept the explanations or assurances of an abuser because he or she is older and has more knowledge or authority. Some older children who know the activity is wrong simply do not know how to deal with the difficult situation. Others have been taught to obey adults without question.

Children living "on their own" are especially vulnerable to those who will provide food, shelter, or money in exchange for sexual activity. Runaways often become prostitutes to provide themselves with basic physical necessities of life.

~ ~ ~

Dr. Finkelhor's model helps us understand the four factors necessary for sexual abuse to occur. The potential abuser must be motivated to have sexual activity with the child and must overcome whatever inhibitions he or she has against this activity. The potential abuser must then have an opportunity to be with the potential victim and must overcome the resistance of the potential victim to the sexual activity.

If any one of these four factors is absent, child sexual abuse will not occur. When all four factors come together, child sexual abuse takes place. Potential abusers become abusers. Potential victims become victims.

Chapter 3.
Who Abuses Children Sexually?

How could an abuser do that to a child? Why would anyone sexually abuse a child?

Answering these questions is not easy. It is often difficult to understand why someone would sexually abuse a child and no one explanation answers the question of why some people become sexually involved with children. Many different reasons are possible.

Most of the reasons that someone abuses a child sexually come down to the fact that the abuser has serious psychological problems. This is not to say that the abuser is "mentally ill." Most abusers are not mentally ill but do have seriously distorted personality traits. Abusers use children to make themselves feel better in some way. They are more interested in satisfying their own needs than in protecting the welfare of their victims

Many types of people sexually abuse children. Although we often think of a sexual abuser as a "dangerous stranger," this is usually not the case. About 80% of child victims are abused by someone they know rather than by a stranger. Most sexual abusers are men, although some are women. Sexual abusers may be of any age from pre-school age to elderly.

Most of what we know about sexual abusers comes from studies of men and boys who abuse children. We have studied and understood them more completely. Therefore, most of this discussion applies primarily to male abusers. Women abuse children, too, but we do not know as much about them. Recently we have also come to realize that many people who sexually abuse children are still children or adolescents themselves.

Ways to Classify Child Sexual Abuse and Abusers

One way to classify child sexual abuse is to consider the context in which it occurs. Abuse may occur as a brief incident, as a part of a continuing relationship outside of the immediate family, or within the immediate family (incest).

Another way to classify child sexual abuse relates to the motivation and acts of the abuser. Most sexual abuse of children is nonviolent. This is usually called child molestation. Sometimes abuse also includes physical violence or threats of violence and is called rape.

Specific characteristics of the abuser may also be important in helping us understand child sexual abuse and abusers. Some abusers are adult men, some are adult women, and some are still children themselves, either males or females. Some abusers have diagnosable mental illnesses or disorders: schizophrenia, bipolar disorder, mental retardation, brain damage, or sociopathy. Others do not.

Special circumstances sometime surround child sexual abuse. Abuse inside correctional institutions and ritual abuse within a cult are two of these special types of abuse.

Common Characteristics of Child Sexual Abusers

Whatever motivations lead an individual to sexually abuse children, these individuals often have characteristics in common.

Many of them were victims of sexual or physical abuse themselves as children.

Most of them are self-centered and think more about satisfying their own needs than about the welfare of the children they abuse.

Most of them "feel bad" if they realize they are harming their victims, but this is not enough to cause them to stop the sexual abuse.

Most sexual abusers of children will continue to abuse until they are stopped by outside intervention.

People who sexually abuse children have serious psychological problems. They can often be helped through professional treatment, however. This treatment usually takes a long time and requires much effort on the part of the abuser. Without treatment, the abuser is most likely to continue abusing children even though he or she may not wish to do so.

The Role of Alcohol and Drugs

Alcohol abuse by the abuser is very commonly associated with child sexual abuse. For abusers who are alcoholics it may be that the personality and interpersonal changes that take place as an individual becomes addicted to alcohol are similar in nature to the type that allow an individual to overcome his internal inhibitions against child sexual abuse.

For other abusers, the use of alcohol at the time of the specific act of sexual abuse allows the abuser to overcome his inhibitions in the area of sexual activity, as in other areas. Sometimes this may be "accidental." A situation may present itself when the abuser is intoxicated that leads to sexual abuse of a child. This is more likely to be the case the first few times an abuser sexually abuses a child.

More often, the abuser intentionally drinks to lower his inhibitions. He drinks to help himself do things he would not be able to do while sober, such as feel relaxed and comfortable in a social situation, express bottled-up anger, or abuse a child sexually. Studies show that incest abusers appear to be the most involved with alcohol of all sex abusers.

~ ~ ~

The next few chapters examine a variety of types of child sexual abusers.

Chapter 4.
Child Molesters

People who abuse children in non-aggressive, non-violent ways, are called **child molesters.**

Child molesters use children to meet their emotional and sexual needs. They are attracted to children as sex objects and are seeking acceptance, companionship, or sexual gratification. Most sexual abuse of children is by child molesters rather than by rapists.

Relationships with other adults, especially sexual relationships, are usually very threatening to both rapists and child molesters. Their reactions to this threat are different, however. The child molester avoids the threat by turning to children as a safer substitute. The rapist denies his fears by striking out and attacking children or adults.

Child molesters are commonly called pedophiles, which means "lovers of children." A pedophile can be anyone who becomes sexually aroused by children, whether or not they are also aroused by adults, but usually refers to the person whose primary sexual interest is in pre-pubescent children. The pedophile may fall anywhere on the continuum, from the individual whose sexual interests are only children, to those who find themselves sexually excited by the image or presence of a child only on rare occasions, however.

Certainly, those who are most interested in children sexually are the ones most likely to abuse them sexually.

American psychologist Nicholas Groth has identified two types of men who molest children: fixated child molesters and regressed child molesters (he was only studying male abusers).

Fixated Child Molesters

Most of us find a wide variety of objects sexually interesting or exciting at one time or another. This may include members of the opposite sex or our own sex, adults of various ages, children of various ages, and even objects or animals. Each of us finds ourselves most easily aroused by individuals of a certain sex, age, physical type, or personality. Most adults find adults of the opposite sex most interesting or exciting.

Some individuals frequently become sexually aroused by children. These individuals, called fixated child molesters, have recurring, intense sexual urges and sexually arousing fantasies involving sexual activity with children who have not yet reached puberty. Fixated child molesters are stuck or "fixated" at a child-like or adolescent level of psychosexual development.

Some fixated child molesters are sexually attracted exclusively to children. Others are also sexually attracted to adults.

Fixated child molesters often report attraction to children of a particular age or sex. Many are sexually aroused by both boys and girls, however. Even though the victim is the same sex as the abuser, the fixated child molester is usually not a homosexual. He does not usually find adult men (or adult women) sexually exciting. He is attracted to boys

42

because they are children, not because they are males.

Some fixated child molesters limit their sexual activity with children to looking at nude children or pictures of nude children, or to exposing their genitals or masturbating in the child's presence. Others may engage in contact or intercourse using varying degrees of force. Most fixated child molesters are friendly, gentle, and attentive to the needs of the child in order to gain access to the child and prevent disclosure of the abuse, however.

Fixated child molesters are people who have never grown up psychologically and socially. They may abuse children because children are the only people with whom they feel comfortable. Or, if the abuser was the victim of child sexual abuse himself, he may sexually abuse children because it allows him to feel like a powerful person instead of a victim.

Fixated child molesters generally begin abusing children in early adolescence, although some do not begin until reaching middle age. They often abuse large numbers of children, in brief incidents, continuing relationships, or incest situations. Sexual contacts are usually planned carefully in advance. Alcohol or drug abuse is not usually related to the sexual abuse.

From a fixated child molester:

Little girls always love my Chihuahuas. The little darlings are so cute when they pretend the puppies are their babies. I have a doll carriage they put them in and push them around. I could watch them play for hours.

The little girl next door was only six when I moved in. She reminded me a lot of my favorite little girl back in Tennessee. I was sorry to have to leave there but some ugly rumors started going around, and anyway she was getting older. Girls seem to   grow up so fast these days.

Now the little girl here, I didn't start touching her until she was almost eight. We played games about keeping secrets, like the candy I would give her, and of course, later, about what we were doing. I never had real sex with her, just got her to rub me until I came. And I always kept my underwear on. I never exposed myself to her. I wouldn't want to hurt her.

Regressed Child Molesters

The primary sexual orientation of regressed child molesters is toward people of their own age. They usually find adults more sexually exciting than children and have developed social skills that allow them to interact with other adults. They often marry and have families of their own.

However, regressed child molesters often have poor resources for handling stress. When these people are under a great deal of stress, they may become overwhelmed. They "regress" or move back to children to meet their emotional needs through sexual activity. They replace their difficult relationships with other adults with involvement with children.

The regressed child molester's sexual abuse of children may occur in cycles. He abuses children primarily when he is experiencing much stress. During periods of low stress, the abuse may stop. He may also have sexual contacts with people his own age during the period of time he is abusing the child. His sexual abuse of children is more likely to be impulsive, at least at first, rather than planned out. Often it takes place when he has been drinking or using drugs. Alcohol is not a cause of the abuse, but its use "allows" the abuser to do things he might not otherwise do.

Regressed child molesters usually choose girls as their victims. The regressed child molester often imagines that the girl is much older than she really is. In his mind, he thinks of her as an adult. Therefore, she becomes an appropriate sexual partner.

Regressed child molesters are often the ones involved in incest. As incest continues, the sexual abuser often abandons his role as parent. The victim gradually takes on responsibilities for keeping the family together and meeting the abuser's needs, so that the abuser's original adult partner becomes almost irrelevant within the family.

From a regressed child molester:

My wife had been ill so long. It had been months since we'd had sex and I just couldn't stand it any more. The only thing in my head was sex, sex, sex. I thought about masturbating but my Bible *is real clear on that. Ever since I was a little kid I've know that's a sin. And I would never go to prostitutes! Diseases, you know.*

My step-daughter and I have always been real close. She knows she's real special to me, and she was right there. I was real gentle with her and she didn't seem to mind. And I'm pretty sure she's too young to get pregnant. It was only a couple of times.

~ ~ ~

In summary, most child sexual abuse is committed by child molesters who abuse children in non-violent ways and are often satisfying emotional as well as sexual needs. These abusers may be either fixated child molesters who select children as their preferred sexual partners, or regressed child molesters who prefer adult sexual partners but turn to children when their preferred partners are not available.

Chapter 5.
Child Rapists

Most sexual abuse of children is nonviolent although sometimes children are forcibly raped. Rape is primarily a form of aggression expressed through sexual acts.

Men who sexually abuse children in violent, aggressive ways are called **rapists**. Rapists use and abuse children through sexual acts mainly to satisfy other needs and desires including power, anger, and sadistic feelings. They may be satisfying sexual needs as well, however.

In addition to studying child molesters Dr. Nicholas Groth has also developed a classification system to identify motives of rapists. Others have since refined or reorganized his classification system but his basic system, with a few additions, remains useful when trying to understand why someone would rape a child.

In Dr. Groth's system the motives for rapes may be divided into three categories: **anger, power,** and **sadism**. Although each incident of rape is usually dominated by one of these motives, some elements of the other two may also be present. Rape is best viewed primarily as an act of aggression but the rapist may also be meeting his sexual needs as well.

The Anger Rapist

The anger rapist attacks children (or adults) as a means of expressing and venting feelings of anger and rage. The rape is often physically brutal with the rapist is taking out his anger at other people, or at frustrating situations, on his victim. His intent is to hurt and debase his victim. Sometimes he makes the victim perform sexual acts that he considers degrading. Anger rapes tend to happen quickly. The rapist often acts without planning and then escapes.

From an anger rapist:

She was wearing a tiny bikini top and flirting with all the boys around the refreshment stand but she wouldn't even talk to me. Called me a dirty old man. Girls always think they can treat me like that! Later I followed her down to the beach. It was dark by then and nobody was around so I grabbed her and shoved her down on the ground. She started to yell but I slapped her hard and told her to shut up or I would really hurt her. I raped her and started slapping her again and that felt even better, but she started screaming so I got out of there. So young, but a bitch already!

The Power Rapist

The power rapist feels inadequate and insecure. His goal in rape is the sexual conquest and control of the victim. This makes him feel powerful. He uses only enough force as is necessary to get what he wants. The power rapist often sees himself as "winning" his victim rather than forcing himself on her. He needs to believe that the victim wanted to have sex with him and even enjoyed it. This way he can feel like an important, desirable, powerful person.

From a power rapist:

Her older sister and I were in high school together. When she turned 14 she was allowed to date so I asked her out. We drove out to the lake. I took a blanket out of the car and we walked along the path till we found an even place where we spread out the blanket. We sat down and talked a while. She seemed like she liked me but turned kind of cold when I started trying to kiss her. I backed off and took my knife out of my pocket. I opened it up and stabbed it into the ground by the blanket a few times and left it there. She let me do what ever I wanted then. She even let me take off her clothes. We had sex. She didn't fight me or anything so I figured she liked it. Then we got dressed and I took her home. I never hurt her or anything. I didn't even say anything about hurting her but she told her mom I raped her and her mom called the cops.

The Sadistic Rapist

Sadistic rapists are very rare but have severe psychological problems. For them, sexuality and aggression become mixed. They get sexual enjoyment and satisfaction from tormenting and injuring victims. Such rapes often end in murder.

From a sadistic child rapist:

When I was in the Navy there were ports where you could find younger girls, anything really. You could do anything you wanted to with them and nobody cared. That was the best.

It was hard after I go home. That day I was just cruising around, thinking about how it had been over there, when I saw her playing by herself near the fairgrounds. I pulled her into the car and took her up in the mountains. I was real disappointed when I realized how young she was 'cause I was looking for someone older, 10 or 12, but I went ahead anyway.

The best was watching her face. It was weird, like I couldn't hear anything at all, like I was in a zone. I could just see her face and see her mouth opening each time I made her scream.

In addition to anger, power, and sadism, men rape for other reasons in certain circumstances:

The Gang Rapist

In gang rapes, each rapist may have a different motive. One may be venting his anger on the victim. Another may be trying to prove his power to the other rapists or to the victim. Still another may be trying to gain acceptance from his buddies.

From a gang rapist:

I really didn't want to do it but I didn't want to look like a wimp. I was the last one to get on her, and really, nothing happened, but I pretended I did it.

The Inmate Rapist

In correctional institutions, rape is one way an inmate claims dominance over another inmate. Although this usually involves sexual acts between two people of the same sex, it has nothing to do with homosexuality. One inmate rapes another to prove that he is more powerful than the other inmate, not because he finds him sexually exciting.

From a juvenile inmate rapist:

It's really not for sex. You just got to make him do it or he won't respect you. Then he'll try to do it to you.

Rape in a War Setting

Combatants may use rape to demonstrate power over, or anger at, those they defeat, or to frighten or humiliate them, or even to purposefully impregnate women and girls and thus leave a lasting reminder of their conquest.

~ ~ ~

While most child sexual abuse is committed by child molesters who abuse children in non-violent ways, sometimes rapists abuse children in violent ways. Their motivations usually relate to anger, power, or sadism but rapists may be satisfying sexual needs as well through these primarily aggressive acts.

51

Chapter 6.
Female Sexual Abusers

For a long time it was assumed that women rarely committed child sexual abuse. Women were viewed as allowing others to abuse their children rather than as abusing children themselves. Recently, we have started to recognize that women do sexually abuse children regularly.

Most sexual abuse of children is still committed by males, however. Studies suggest that probably only 20% of boys who are sexually abused and 5% of girls who are sexually abused are abused by females.

Not very much is known about women who sexually abuse children. They often seem to come from chaotic, highly dysfunctional backgrounds involving physical, sexual, and substance abuse. Women abusers usually have sexual contact with children during a continuing relationship or during incest. Their victims are usually boys, although they sometimes abuse girls. These types of abuse are not reported often, even when they are discovered.

Even less is known about girls who abuse children although they are thought to have commonly been sexually abused themselves in highly traumatic ways. Most are likely to engage in other disruptive or delinquent acts as well as sexual abuse.

Women and girls who sexually abuse children are usually "caretakers" for them, most often mothers, stepmothers, older sisters, or babysitters. They may sexually abuse children in more subtle ways than men do so that the abuse may be masked through the guise of care taking activities.

Women sexual abusers are often single. If they are married, their husbands are often gone from the home or emotionally distant. They may choose partners who recreate their own chaotic families of origin. These women are usually very possessive and overprotective of their victims, and are very immature themselves. They probably abuse children primarily to satisfy emotional rather than sexual needs.

From a female sexual abuser:

When he was little he always slept with me when his dad was gone, which was a lot of the time. I hate being alone. After he was asleep, I would rub myself on his legs. Sometimes he would wake up but he really didn't know what was going on. I would just tell him to rub me with his knee 'cause it felt so good. Then when he was older he wouldn't sleep with me anymore.

~ ~ ~

At present, little is known about the frequency of child sexual abuse by women. Most female abusers seem to be satisfying emotional as much as sexual needs through the abuse, which is often carried out in the context of caretaking activities.

Chapter 7.
Children Who Abuse Other Children

As is true with most studies of child sexual abusers, most of our current knowledge about children who sexually abuse other children comes from studies of male abusers. Child sexual abuse by female children is rarely reported, much less studied.

Society often does not view the acts of child or adolescent sexual abusers as serious. Professionals, parents, and even authorities are often reluctant to label a juvenile as a "child molester" or "sex offender."

Recent studies have shown, however, that sexual abusers often begin their "careers" as teenagers, or even earlier. Perhaps as many as one-half of all child sexual abusers have committed their first abuse by the time they are 18 years of age, many by the age of eight or nine. Sexual abuse by children can represent the early stages of serious psychological and behavior problems that develop and continue into adult life.

However, just as most sexually abused children do not go on to abuse others, most juveniles who abuse others do not go on to abuse children once they themselves become adults. Unfortunately, we still have no good way of knowing who will continue to abuse and who will not.

Children who are involved as abusers in more than one incident of abuse, those who abuse others violently, and those who are in their teens when they abuse seem more likely to continue sexual abuse of children once they themselves become adults.

Studies suggest that there are many factors that lead children to abuse other children, and there are many paths to abuse. No one set of factors or one developmental pattern is seen in all children who abuse.

Several systems for classifying boys who abuse children sexually have been proposed. Many professionals find a seven-category system called the PHASE Typology developed by American psychologists Michael O'Brien and Walter Bera (and named after the organization where the two men worked) to be useful.

Drs. O'Brien and Bera emphasized that no one explanation of child sexual abuse applies to every adolescent abuser. In their seven categories we can also see the early development of the various types of adults who sexually abuse children.

The **Naive Experimenter,** is usually young (age 11 through 14) and has little previous history of trouble. He gets along well with other adolescents, but tends to be sexually inexperienced and naïve. He engages in a single or a few isolated acts of sexual exploration with a younger child, using no force or threats. His motivation appears to be one of learning, exploration, and experimenting with his newly developing sexual feelings.

The **Under-socialized Child Exploiter** usually plays alone or with younger children, who admire and accept him. With peers, he feels inadequate and insecure. The family often shows a pattern of an over-involved mother and a cold or distant father. His motivation for the abuse is usually an attempt to achieve intimacy, or to increase his sense of self-importance.

From an under-socialized child exploiter:

There was my younger brother and two other boys who were his friends in the club. I was the president and got to make the rules. They would do anything I said. It was great. We spent a lot of time playing in our fort in the woods behind our house. Almost every day we would do our "secret stuff" which was to go behind the fort and pee and then I would have them play with each others' wieners. I never touched them and never had them touch me, just made them play with each other. They did anything I said.

The **Pseudo-socialized Child Exploiter** appears to be socially confident and secure with peers. He generally is an older adolescent with good social skills and no history of trouble. He is often bright and a hard worker. He may have been the victim of early childhood abuse or neglect of some type himself. His abusive behavior often lasts over a long period of time. He views his behavior as intimate, non-coercive, and something that the other child participates in willingly. He rationalizes his behavior and rarely shows a sense of guilt or remorse. His motivation appears to be a self-centered exploitation of a vulnerable child to gain sexual pleasure for himself.

From a pseudo-sexualized child exploiter:

I couldn't do it every night because it took too long and I needed the sleep. My sister never knew, so it wasn't like I was hurting her. She never woke up because I was really careful and took my time. After everybody was asleep I would slip down the hall to her room and sit by her bed. Slowly, slowly I would slip my hand under the covers and under her nightgown and then I would penetrate her, just a little. It was really exciting! It was hard because I had to slip out again and go back to my room before I came.

The **Sexual Aggressive**, is often a sociable, likable child with good peer social skills. He is often the product of a disorganized and abusive family and probably has a long history of antisocial behaviors, including fighting, truancy, vandalism, and substance abuse. The abuse typically involves use of threats of violence to obtain sexual compliance. His motivation appears to be the use of sex to gain a feeling of power through domination, to express anger, or to dominate and humiliate his victim. Such individuals sometimes learn to become sexually aroused only in the expression of violence.

The **Sexual Compulsive**, engages in compulsive sexual behavior such as exhibitionism, window peeping, or obscene phone calling. The offense is usually a planned, solitary activity which reduces a state of tension or anxiety and makes him "feel better." He usually comes from a family where the parents have great difficulty expressing intimacy or any other emotion. His motivation is the feeling of release from tension that accompanies his compulsive sexual activity.

From a sexual compulsive:

I got caught the first time when I was 15 but I had been doing it a couple of years by then. I would just walk around the neighborhood and peep in windows at night. Mom never noticed where I was so it was easy to sneak out. I only watched women or girls. Sometimes just watching them doing something like getting dressed or undressed was enough. Sometimes I would masturbate while I watched them. I liked it best when they would walk around half dressed, like in a slip or just panties. That was better than completely naked.

The **Disturbed Impulsive**, usually has serious mental or emotional difficulties. The sexual abuse is usually impulsive, unpredictable, and may involve unusual or bizarre sexual acts towards children, peers, or adults.

From a disturbed impulsive abuser:

We got off the bus together every day after school and sometimes she would talk to me like she liked me. I thought a lot about all the things I could do to her. Then I saw her at a party one night. She was drunk. I took her out back and grabbed a pop bottle and broke the neck off and raped her with it. She was screaming and there was blood everywhere. It was great! I didn't even care when they called the cops.

The **Group Influenced Sex Abuser**, is usually a younger teen who has rarely been in trouble in the past. The sexual abuse occurs with a peer group present. The abuser tries to explain his behavior by blaming the victim or other participants in the group. The motivation can come from peer pressure or expectations that he go along with their sexual behavior or from an attempt to gain attention and approval from peers.

~ ~ ~

Many child sexual abusers carry out their first acts of abuse while still children themselves. As with older abusers, patterns of abuse and motivating factors vary widely among abusers.

Chapter 8.
Other Types of Abusers

Sociopaths or Opportunistic Child Sexual Abusers

A sociopath is an individual with an "Antisocial Personality Disorder." This type of person is extremely self-centered and cares little for the rules of society or for the welfare of others. His or her own desires are more important. Such individuals are sometimes described as having "no conscience."

The sociopath may be a charming, clever, and interesting person. Often he becomes involved in criminal activities. Although rapists and child molesters with motives described in previous chapters are often sociopaths, other motives for child sexual abuse also occur among this group of abusers.

A sociopath often craves variety and excitement. Having sex with children may be just one of the many types of sexual activities he tries "for kicks." He may not be especially interested in children as sexual objects, but rather, may be interested in the excitement of a new experience. Other sociopaths may sexually abuse children simply because children are easily available to satisfy their sexual needs.

Sociopaths usually become involved in brief incidents of sexual abuse, although involvement in continuing relationships or incest is also possible.

From a sociopath abuser:

I had never raped anybody and I started wondering what it would be like. I rode my bike over to the next suburb, heading for the mall, but then I went by a high school and students were just coming out into this huge parking lot. I put my bike down and walked around. I wasn't much older than them so I blended in OK. After the cars had thinned out, this girl came out by herself. She was pretty cute so I followed her to her car. She got in, then turned around and started messing with stuff in the back seat. I started walking up to her side of the car holding my knife down close to my leg. Then I saw that the door on the passenger side was unlocked, so I went around and jumped in. I grabbed her arm and held the knife against her ribs and told her, "Stay quiet and drive where I tell you and I won't hurt you."

You wouldn't believe what she did! She started hitting at me and yelling and punched me right in the face! It didn't hurt a lot but it split my lip and blood started going everywhere. She kept screaming at me and hitting and people started coming toward us. I jumped out and lit out on my bike. I got away but I didn't get to rape her. It was still pretty exciting though!

Mentally Ill, Mentally Retarded, or Brain Damaged Child Sexual Abusers

Mental retardation, brain damage (caused by accident, stroke, a degenerative brain condition such as Alzheimer's disease, or other physical injury to the brain), and serious mental illness such as Schizophrenia or Bipolar Disorder

62

(manic-depressive illness) can cause serious distortions in thinking and judgment. Sometimes this leads mentally retarded, brain damaged, or mentally ill individuals to become sexually involved with children. The sexual abuse is usually closely associated with their psychiatric problems.

Most sexual abusers do not have these types of psychiatric problems, however. And most mentally retarded, brain damaged, or mentally ill individuals do not abuse children.

From a brain damaged abuser:

It's OK here at the hospital except they keep taking my pictures away. I carry them in my wallet and don't show them to anybody. I just like to look at them sometimes. There's nothing wrong with them. They come out of the ads in Sunday papers: sweet little boys in bathing suits, or shorts and shirts. Not even underwear or anything. They keep taking them away though, but I can always get more.

From a schizophrenic abuser:

I was saving them. I didn't want my little girls to go to hell. I loved them. You know, if they had sex with boys they would die and go to hell. I had to save them when they were young so that's why I had sex with them.

Ritual Child Sexual Abuse within a Cult

Rape or other sexual abuse of children sometimes occurs as an acceptable, and even required, part of the rituals within a cult. A cult leader may require his followers to participate in ritual child sexual abuse as a way of reinforcing his dominance over them. Ritual abusers within a cult may be trying to demonstrate their loyalty to the cult or to the cult leader. Ritual abusers may also be trying to "educate" children growing up within the cult to increase their loyalty and dependence on the cult through fear and domination.

~ ~ ~

Not all child sexual abuse or abusers fit neatly into categories. Abuse by sociopaths, by mentally ill individuals, by those who are mentally retarded or brain damaged, and ritual abuse within a cult all require special consideration.

Chapter 9.
Treatment for Child Sexual Abusers

WHY TREAT THE ABUSER?

Most people want to understand and help children victimized by sexual abuse. But what about helping the abuser, the person who has caused all the pain and emotional turmoil for the child victim and his or her family?

Sexual abuse situations are often highly emotional. Most people want to punish the abuser severely: "Lock him up and throw away the key!" Treatment is just letting the abuser get off easy. Why would we bother helping the abuser?

In fact, many reasons for helping the abuser exist. These involve concerns for the abuser himself or herself, concerns for the victim of the sexual abuse, and concerns for society in general, especially for children the abuser could encounter as potential victims in the future.

Treating the abuser benefits the abuser

Some people want to help sexual abusers for humanitarian reasons. We may believe that an individual, no matter what crimes he or she has committed, no matter what injuries he or she has caused, is still a fellow human being who deserves our understanding, compassion, and assistance.

It may be easier to look at the abuser this way if we remember what statistics tell us about abusers. Studies suggest that most sexual abusers were themselves victims of child sexual abuse. If we think of the abuser as a former victim, we may be more willing to try to understand the difficulties that have led to the abuser's behavior.

From a more personal standpoint, we may wish to help the abuser because the abuser is someone we care about very much. In an abuse situation, the abuser is rarely a stranger. He or she may be a close friend, a husband or wife, a daughter or son, a sister or brother. This is often the case in incest situations where emotional, financial, and personal ties with the abuser remain strong. Family members may not be willing to "write off" the abuser, simply because he or she has victimized one of them.

Treating the abuser benefits the victim

Another reason to provide treatment for the abuser is for the benefit of his or her victim. This can occur in several ways.

If the abuser knows that treatment is available, the chances are increased (although still rather small) that he or she will seek help on his or her own, thus ending the abuse.

Additionally, people (including the victim) who know about the abuse are more likely to report it if they know that help is available for the abuser, not just punishment.

This is particularly true when the abuser is a friend or family member as is the case in 80% of all child sexual abuse situations.

When the child victim knows that, by reporting the abuse, he or she has helped the abuser "get well," the victim is less likely to feel guilty about disclosing the abuse.

Treating the abuser also emphasizes two important messages to the victim. First: the sexual abuse happened because something was wrong with the abuser, not with the victim. Second: the victim did the right thing in disclosing the sexual abuse so that the abuser could get the help he or she needs to live a better life.

Finally, involving the abuser in appropriate individual, family, or group therapy is often needed to promote successful treatment of the victim. This is especially true in incest situations. Helping the victim of incest ideally involves treating the whole family system, not just the child who was abused.

Treating the abuser benefits society

Concerns about benefits to society in general also lead us to treat the abuser. From a philosophical standpoint, improving the mental health of any member of society improves the overall quality of our society. From a more practical standpoint, treating the abuser usually reduces the risk of that person sexually abusing other children in the future.

The laws of our society do not permit sexual abusers to be "locked up forever." At some point, the sexual abuser will return to society, if he or she were ever "put away" to begin with. If the abuser's mental health has not improved while he or she was "locked up," the abuser is probably going to abuse others once he or she is released. The abuser may even abuse other, more vulnerable, inmates while incarcerated. Thus we prevent others from becoming victims by helping the abuser change his or her abusive behavior.

Finally, from an even more practical standpoint, it is much cheaper to treat a sexual abuser on an outpatient basis, or even on a short-term inpatient basis, than it is to send the abuser to prison. Our main concern is in preventing the abuser from victimizing others in the future, rather than merely punishing him or her for past behavior. It is much cheaper to let abusers remain free on probation while they receive appropriate treatment (and close supervision). Then they can continue working and supporting their families, rather than become a burden to taxpayers. Certainly such treatment is not appropriate for all sexual abusers, but for some it is.

Thus, a number of valid reasons for treating the abuser all point to the fact that we cannot just treat the victim and ignore the abuser if we want to solve problems related to child sexual abuse.

TREATMENT FOR THE ABUSER

Different types of sexual abusers need different types of treatment. Right now, some sexual abusers simply cannot be treated successfully with our current treatment procedures. Treatment success is very low or nonexistent for individuals of certain personality types, such as sociopaths, or for certain types of sexual abusers, such as sadistic rapists. For these people, incarceration for as long a period as possible, and close monitoring after their release, is the only practical solution at present. Perhaps in the future we will find new and better treatment methods, which can be more helpful in these situations as well.

Other sexual abusers can benefit from treatment of a variety of types. The first step to finding the right treatment is a thorough assessment of the abuser. Assessment procedures identify those who can be helped through treatment and identify which types of treatment will meet their specific needs most effectively. Then treatment can be tailored to meet the specific needs and abilities of the individual abuser.

Many sexual abusers express great remorse about the abuse after it is disclosed. They assure everyone that the problem has already been solved once the abuse is disclosed, sometimes citing newly found religious faith. They will never ever do it again, they claim.

Studies indicate that this is not true. If sexual abusers could solve their problems on their own and stop abusing children without professional intervention, they would have done it. Almost no sexual abuser stops his or her abuse without some type of outside intervention.

Certainly many sources of assistance can help abusers avoid future abuse. Religious faith, family support, and even self-help measures may all be helpful. None of these, by themselves, appears to be enough, however. More is needed.

For some sexual abusers, exposure of their actions, and the threat of legal prosecution, may be enough to prevent future abuse. The potential for abuse is always very close to the surface for these individuals, however. Abusers frequently take extreme risks, even when it seems like the threat of being caught and prosecuted would stop them.

Successful treatment of a sexual abuser requires a great amount of motivation and effort on the part of the abuser. Some individuals can be successfully treated through outpatient therapy. Others require a period of inpatient treatment, followed by outpatient treatment.

What is successful treatment?

When we talk about successful treatment of sexual abusers, we are really talking about "control" of the problem. We are not talking about a "cure." The tendency toward sexual abuse of children can be viewed like the diseases of diabetes or alcoholism. Right now, we know no way to "cure" these difficulties. With proper treatment, we can keep these diseases under control. The problem itself never goes away. It remains a life-long threat for the person who is a diabetic, an alcoholic, or a sexual abuser.

It is hard to know when the treatment for a child sexual abuser is a success. What we really mean when we say that treatment has been successful is that the person has not been reported abusing anyone again. Therefore, much of our knowledge about "success" is limited because we rarely know whether the abuser has really stopped abusing children. We only know that he or she has not been reported abusing anyone. In spite of these problems, some interventions do seem to reduce incidents of abuse by abusers receiving treatment.

Many types of treatments exist. These may be divided into **physical treatments, physiological retraining procedures,** and **psychotherapy.**

Physical Treatments

Physical Treatment procedures are usually considered drastic and are rarely used, except in special situations. Surgical castration of male sex offenders is a solution that has been suggested from time to time. Occasionally it is practiced. A related but less drastic procedure called "chemical castration" involves the use of sex hormone treatment to reduce sexual urges and aggressive behaviors in males. The administration of major tranquilizers (like Thorazine), which reduce sexual interest or sexual ability as a side effect, has also occasionally been tried.

While these procedures are sometimes useful, particularly with individuals who have been involved in violent sexual crimes, they address only the sexual aspects of sexual abuse. As we have seen, child sexual abuse involves many needs, drives, and behaviors, which are not all related to physical sexual gratification. Therefore, it is unrealistic to believe that procedures that treat only the sexual aspects of the abuse will solve the problems that led the individual to abuse children sexually. All of the physical treatments also have potentially harmful side effects and raise ethical issues for the treating professionals and for society.

Physiological Retraining

Physiological retraining procedures generally involve changing the abuser's reactions to sexual stimuli involved in child sexual abuse. The goal of retraining is to reduce the abuser's sexual arousal to children.

During one method of physiological retraining called "orgasmic reconditioning" the abuser learns to become sexually aroused by appropriate sexual stimuli (adults) rather than inappropriate sexual stimuli (children).

During this treatment the abuser is encouraged to masturbate while imagining or looking at pictures of adults in sexual scenes. The abuser may also receive mild electric shocks when he or she becomes sexually excited while looking at sexual pictures of children. Instruments similar to biofeedback or lie detector equipment are used to measure sexual excitement.

Another physiological retraining procedure has been used with exhibitionists, or "flashers," who derive sexual satisfaction from exposing their genitals to strangers.

In this self-administered aversive training procedure, abusers carry a bottle of foul-smelling liquid with them at all times. When they find themselves in situations where they feel the urge to expose themselves, they smell the contents of the vial. This leads them to associate exposure situations with immediate unpleasant consequences, rather than pleasant, sexually gratifying consequences. The result is to reduce their desire to expose themselves.

As with physical treatments, physiological reconditioning can have beneficial effects for sexual abusers. Also like physical treatments, physiological reconditioning usually addresses only certain of the factors leading to child sexual abuse. By themselves, these treatments are not likely to provide lasting successful results. Many other psychological and emotional factors as well as the sexual aspects of child sexual abuse must be addressed if treatment is to be successful.

Issues related to the ethics of behavioral change procedures, and the lasting effectiveness of these procedures also arise.

Psychotherapy

In psychotherapy the abuser can address the sexual abuse itself, his or her sexual needs, and any emotional needs that led to the abuse.

Many different styles and approaches to psychotherapy exist but the main goal is always to help the abuser change

72

his or her behavior so that he or she no longer abuses. As a first step, the therapist usually tries to help the abuser identify and admit the full scope of the abuse, and take responsibility for his or her actions.

Therapy also usually helps the abuser understand what led him or her to abuse and how the abuse has affected others, especially the victim, while helping the abuser develop understanding and concern for past and potential victims. If the abuser was previously a victim of abuse, the effects of these events can be addressed in therapy.

Finally, therapy helps the abuser learn new and more appropriate ways of meeting his or her own needs, rather than continuing to abuse children, as well as helping the abuser develop better ways of controlling his or her own actions.

Training in life management skills are often included as a supplement to psychotherapy. Training in basic sex education, sensitivity to the thoughts and feelings of others, problem solving skills, social and communication skills, assertiveness, stress and anger management, emotional expression, and parenting skills can be included as needed.

Counseling for drug or alcohol problems and arrangements for vocational rehabilitation, physical therapy, spiritual counseling, or other needs can also be coordinated with psychotherapy. Physiological retraining or even some form of physical treatment may also be included with psychotherapy as a part of the overall treatment program.

Psychotherapeutic intervention may be provided through individual therapy, couples or marital therapy, family therapy, or group therapy, including self-help groups. A particularly interesting and effective self-help approach involving groups for former victims, family members, and abusers, has been started in California through self-help groups called Parents United and Daughters and Sons United.

Treating abusers with special needs

Special issues arise when dealing with certain abusers. These include children who abuse, female abusers, mentally ill abusers, mentally retarded or brain damaged abusers, and sociopaths.

Much sexual abuse is performed by individuals who are not yet themselves eighteen years old. Children as young as four or five sometimes abuse other children. Often we try to ignore, forgive, or excuse away the young sexual abuser. Abuse by a child or adolescent may also be viewed as "normal sex play" or "innocent curiosity." We think that it is not really important, not serious, or "merely a phase they're going through." This is a great mistake. Sexual abuse by children and adolescents should be taken very seriously.

Children who abuse other children may be doing serious damage to their victims. And often, children who abuse become teenagers who abuse and then become adults who abuse.

Most sex offenders in prison report that they first began sexually abusing others in their pre-teen or early teen years. A pattern of sexual abuse that begins in these early years is not likely to decrease or "go away" as the child gets older. Quite the opposite takes place. The sexual abuse is likely to happen more often and take more serious forms as the abuser gets older.

The child or adolescent sexual abuser needs immediate, intensive treatment designed specifically for young sexual abusers. This should involve a thorough assessment of the possibility that the abuser has also been a victim of sexual abuse. If this has been the case, treatment should also include help for other problems resulting from victimization.

Female sexual abusers are frequently dismissed as causing little damage. This may be because we do not view females as being sexually threatening in our society. However, just like male abusers, female abusers can harm victims greatly. They are also experiencing serious emotional difficulties themselves. They should be involved in treatment for the same reasons that apply to male abusers but treatment programs for female abusers need to be tailored to their specific needs. Sometimes these needs are similar to the needs of male abusers. Often the needs of female abusers are different.

Mentally ill, mentally retarded, or brain damaged sexual abusers present special problems and have special treatment needs. Sometimes a mentally ill or "psychotic" individual, someone with schizophrenia, bipolar disorder (manic-depressive illness) or another mental illness that causes him or her to lose contact with reality and to think in "crazy" ways, sexually abuses children. When the psychosis itself is treated and controlled, usually through medication, the sexual abuse may be controlled as well. For other individuals, the problem with psychosis and the problem with sexual abuse are two different and distinct sets of difficulties. Then each needs to be treated separately. Close supervision must often be a major part of the treatment of mentally ill abusers.

When the abuser is mentally retarded or seriously brain damaged, intervention must depend more on external control than treatment. Certainly, mentally retarded or brain damaged individuals have the same needs, desires, and emotional difficulties that are found in the general population, including the general population of sex abusers. Some of the same treatment approaches may be useful. In the long run however, prevention of future abuse must depend more on close supervision than on expecting them to change their behaviors because their disorders may seriously compromise their abilities to control their behaviors appropriately.

Sociopaths have traditionally been resistant to treatment of any type. Until methods of treatment that are consistently effective for such individuals emerge, close supervision remains the only potentially effective approach to preventing them from abusing further.

Finding treatment

Finding help for an abuser is often difficult. Many mental health professionals do not treat sexual abusers because they do not have the specialized training to deal effectively with the problems which led a person to abuse children sexually. Others choose not to treat abusers because of their personal feelings about child sexual abuse.

It is important to find a mental health professional who wants to treat sexual abusers and who has the specialized skills to do this. The professional should also have substantial experience working with abusers. Such professionals are found most often in residential treatment programs for sexual abusers.

It is hard to find such professionals who provide treatment on an outpatient basis. The local community mental health center, social services agency, or rape crisis center may be able to provide the names of local mental health professionals who treat sexual abusers.

Keep in mind that any professional contacted about child sexual abuse will probably report the abuse to the authorities as they are required by law to do this. If the abuse is recent, criminal charges may be filed against the abuser or other legal action may be taken to protect the child from further abuser. However, authorities are usually more interested in preventing further abuse than in punishing past actions. If the abuser is seeking treatment, this is usually taken into consideration in any legal proceedings.

Deciding whether to seek help for the abuser is certainly difficult. Help is available. Often successful treatment is possible but there is never a guarantee of its success. The only guarantee is that the abuser will not stop abusing children without treatment.

~ ~ ~

Treating abusers is a final but important part of solving the problem of child sexual abuse in our society. Treatment is available to help abusers who really want to change their abusive behavior, although successful treatment results in "control" of the problem, not in a "cure." Problems leading an individual to abuse a child sexually require life-long treatment to remain successful.

Afterword

This book has addressed the questions "Why would anyone sexually abuse a child?" and "How can child sexual abuse happen?" as well as "How can child sexual abusers stop abusing?"

Our society is just beginning to find answers to these difficult questions. As studies and research on child sexual abuse continue, hopefully someday more definitive answers will prevent any child from ever becoming a victim of child sexual abuse.

Did you find this book helpful?

Please let others know about it.

Share it with someone today. Write a review. Mention it on your blog or in your social media messages.

Thank you for your assistance in letting others know this information is available.

Do you know someone who was the victim of child sexual abuse?

Find help and healing
in Dr. Lynn Daugherty's classic bestseller,

Why Me?
Help for Victims of Child Sexual Abuse
(Even if they are adults now)

Available in paperback or as an ebook.

Additional Resources

Look for these books at your public library, or purchase them from your online bookseller or your local bookstore. Find out more about these and other resources at our website:

www.cleananpress.com

This listing of books is not an endorsement of any of them or of the information they contain. You should learn as much as possible about child sexual abuse for yourself, but always examine information critically and tailor it to your own individual needs.

Information about child sexual abusers

A. Nicholas Groth. *Men Who Rape: The Psychology of The Offender*. (Basic Books, 1979). Classic, and still relevant, information about men who rape adults and children.

Michele Elliott. *Female Sexual Abuse of Children*. (The Guilford Press, 1994). Provides some of the first detailed information about female abusers and their victims.

Phil Rich. *Understanding, Assessing and Rehabilitating Juvenile Sexual Offenders, Second Edition*. (Wiley, 2011). Current information about juvenile abusers.

Anna Salter. *Predators: Pedophiles, Rapists, And Other Sex Offenders*. (Basic Books, 2004). Profiles abusers of adults and children and suggests ways to protect against them.

Books to help parents protect their children

Leigh Baker. *Protecting Your Children From Sexual Predators*. St. Martin's Press, 2005. Helps parents protect their children from various types of sexual predators (offenders who repeatedly target children for violent sexual abuse).

Robin Sax. *Predators and Child Molesters: What Every Parent Needs to Know to Keep Kids Safe*. (Prometheus Books, 2009). Recognizing predators, talking to kids about risks, identifying potential problems, reporting sexual abuse, going to court, and recovery from abuse.

Carla Van Dam. *Identifying Child Molesters: Preventing Child Sexual Abuse by Recognizing the Patterns of the Offenders* (Routledge, 2001). Helps parents recognize and avoid potential child molesters.

About the Author

Clinical psychologist Dr. Lynn Daugherty is an award-winning author of the classic bestseller **Why Me? Help for Victims of Child Sexual Abuse (Even if they are adults now)**, currently in its 4th edition. An internationally respected expert on child sexual abuse, she has been bringing hope and healing to victims and their families for more than twenty-five years.

Now, in response to the question, "Why would anyone abuse children sexually?" Dr. Daugherty presents basic information about abuse and sex offenders in this current book, **Child Molesters, Child Rapists, and Child Sexual Abuse**.

Another of Dr. Daugherty's books, **Voices of Survivors**, a collection of stories told by former victims of child sexual abuse, excerpted from *Why Me? Help for Victims of Child Sexual Abuse (Even if they are adults now)*, designed to reassure other victims that they are not alone, is available as an ebook.

Dr. Daugherty's most recent ebook, **Listening and Talking to Your Sexually Abused Child**, guides parents' communication as they help a child heal from child sexual abuse.

A Selection from . . .

Why Me?

**Help for Victims
of Child Sexual Abuse
(Even if they are adults now)**

by Dr. Lynn Daugherty

Table of Contents

Chapter Four.
The effects of child sexual abuse on the victim and the victim's family

Child sexual abuse affects the way a victim thinks, feels and acts. **Confusion** is often the victim's first reaction. Many times the victim also feels strong and frightening emotions. The victim may come to believe bad things about him or herself and about other people because of the sexual abuse. As a result, the behavior of the victim may change in many ways.

This chapter discusses many of the ways a victim thinks, feels and acts as a result of child sexual abuse. It also discusses the reactions of the victim's family.

Confusion

Surprise and confusion are often the first reactions of a victim of child sexual abuse. He or she thinks, "What is going on? Is this right or wrong? What should I do? Will it happen again? Should I tell someone? Why do I feel so funny? Why is this happening to me?"

It is natural to be confused when something happens that you don't understand. Children cannot be expected to know how to respond to sexual abuse, unless they have been taught what to do. The child's confusion is one weapon the abuser uses against the child to take advantage of him or her.

Even after the child victim grows up, some confusion about the sexual abuse may remain. That is one reason why it is helpful for a victim to learn as much as possible about child sexual abuse. In this way, the victim often finds answers to many of the questions he or she has had for so long.

In addition to being confused about the sexual abuse, the victim may also be confused about the many different emotions he or she has been feeling. It is confusing to feel so many emotions at the same time. Sorting them out and understanding each one is hard. This chapter will help you make sense of some of the emotions you may have felt.

Many times victims of child sexual abuse worry about the emotions they feel. Sometimes they are frightened by them or ashamed of them. It is normal for victims to have many, many emotions: some pleasant, some unpleasant, and some even frightening to think about or to feel. All of these emotions are normal reactions to being a victim of child sexual abuse.

Just what kinds of feelings or emotions do children have when they are victims of sexual abuse? Children often feel **anger**, **fear**, **shame** and **guilt**. Let's talk about each one of these feelings.

Anger

The child victim often feels anger. The victim may be angry at the abuser because of what he or she is doing. The victim may be angry at him or herself for not knowing what to do about the abuse. The victim may be angry at his or her parents for not preventing the abuse or for not taking action to stop it from happening again. The victim may be angry at anybody and everybody because of what has happened.

Often, when a girl is being abused by her father or stepfather, she tries to tell her mother what is happening. Many times her mother is afraid to become involved because she doesn't know what to do. Sometimes the mother will say she doesn't believe her daughter, or that what is happening is the daughter's fault. Then the mother will not do anything to stop the sexual abuse.

Other times the mother tries to stop it, but she cannot without telling other people. Then she may do nothing because she is ashamed of what her husband is doing or she may be afraid of breaking up the family. So the abuse continues. The victim in this kind of situation often feels much anger toward her mother.

Some victims are frightened by their own anger. They are afraid that if they start to express their anger, it will be so strong that they will do something violent.

Fear

Many children who are the victims of sexual abuse feel fear. There are many things to fear. The child may be afraid of being hurt by the abuser, especially if the abuser threatens this. The child may fear that he or she has been physically damaged in some way by the sexual abuse. The child may be afraid of not being believed if he or she does tell someone about the abuse. The child may be afraid of some harm coming to the offender or to someone else in the family if the abuse is discovered.

The child may be afraid the family will break up or may be afraid of losing the friendship and love of the abuser or of another family member. The child may be afraid of being blamed for the abuse. The child may be afraid of being arrested or punished for having done something wrong. The child may be afraid of having to talk to strangers about the abuse or of testifying in court if charges are filed against the abuser. The child may be frightened of being abused again.

Sometimes there are so many fears that the child begins to feel fearful all the time without being able to identify exactly what it is that is feared. This constant unidentified fear makes life very difficult for the child. Sometimes these feelings of fear and anxiety stay with the victim for a long time.

Shame

Shame is another emotion the child victim often feels. He or she may feel "dirty." The victim may feel he or she is the only person such a thing has ever happened to and that he or she is different from everyone else. The victim fears that other people will find out how different, or how dirty, or how bad he or she really is. The victim believes no one would like or care about him or her if anyone knew about the sexual abuse.

Guilt

The child victim of sexual abuse frequently feels guilty for what is happening. The victim may believe that the sexual abuse is his or her fault. This is especially true if the abuse was ever pleasurable or if the abuser gave the child special rewards. The victim may believe that he or she did something to bring on the abuse or feel guilty because he or she did not try hard enough to stop the abuse. The victim may feel guilty for any good feelings toward the abuser or for bad feelings toward family members who were not helpful enough.

If the victim does report the abuse, many of the results can cause feelings of guilt in the victim. Sometimes the abuser is put in prison. Other times, when the abuser is a parent, the marriage may end in divorce and the family may be split up. The victim often feels guilty, believing that he or she has caused all of this to happen. This is especially true if other family members blame the victim.

All of these emotions are common reactions of children who have been sexually abused. Perhaps you can identify some of these emotions in the victims who told their stories in Chapter Two. Have you felt any of these emotions? Do you worry about having these emotions? Each person has a right to his or her own feelings. All of these emotions, and many others, are normal reactions to sexual abuse.

Other problems, in addition to strong and unpleasant emotions, can result from child sexual abuse. Some of the **physical** and **psychological** problems that child sexual abuse can cause are discussed next . . . .

For more information about the effects of child sexual abuse, ways to begin recovering from these effects, and basic information about child sexual abuse and abusers, as well as stories from former victims . . .

Why Me?
Help for Victims of Child Sexual Abuse
(Even if they are adults now)

Available in paperback or as an ebook.

~

To read experiences of former victims and know you are not alone . . .

Child Molestation Stories
Voices of Survivors
of Child Sexual Abuse

Available in paperback or as an ebook.

~

To strengthen your relationship with your child as you start on your journey to recovery . . .

Listening and Talking
to Your Sexually Abused Child

Available in paperback or as an ebook.

www.ingramcontent.com/pod-product-compliance
Lightning Source LLC
Chambersburg PA
CBHW032031290526
45786CB00011B/1350